the wanderer

Kenzie Whipple

the wanderer © 2021 Kenzie Whipple

All rights reserved.

No part of this publication may be
reproduced, stored in a retrieval system, or
transmitted, in any form or by any means,
electronic, mechanical, photocopying,
recording or otherwise, without the prior
written permission of the presenters.

Kenzie Whipple asserts the moral right to
be identified as author of this work.

Presentation by *BookLeaf Publishing*

Web: www.bookleafpub.com

E-mail: info@bookleafpub.com

ISBN : 9789357447355

First edition 2021

DEDICATION

To the people behind the poems - you made me.

Phoenix

I slept, and as I slept, I dreamt
Of a past long gone by
I saw myself
Younger
With a look of innocence in my eye
I knew that pain was to follow
And heartbreak
And sorrow
And tears
I tried to stop myself from touching the
heartbreak,
Reaching past through the years.

I could not warn her enough
I could not stop myself, the fool,
I still was broken and crying
There was nothing I could do

As I watched
My heart seemed to turn to ashes
And my pain went up in flames
I changed before my own eyes
Nothing was the same

From the ashes there arose a warrior

Whose heart was beating strong
Who was fierce and independent
She didn't let others string her along.

I realized that I am the warrior
I have conquered the flames, broken through the
night
I am the raging fire
Watch as I ignite

My scars and pain make me stronger
I am a player in no game
For I am the warrior maiden
And Phoenix is my name.

Rebel Stride

The words don't come easily
I have to catch them one by one
But I need a way to let it all out
To show the world what I've become

I am no perfect daughter
I walk with a rebel stride
An angel that waltzes with demons
The fear that once ruled me has died

You think that you know me
Look into my eyes and see
I'm running wild with the fire
And the flames are dancing free

Gold

I am the gold
That glows and fades
Day by day.

I am the shine that brightens
And then disappears.
I am the fingertips of dawn
I am the gold.

I do not glitter
I do not sparkle
I shine

The night follows me
Wherever I go
Shrouded in black
Darkness is my cloak

I am hope, for no matter how long
Night may be,
I return.

Jag är guldet som glöder och blecknar dag för
dag.
Jag är lysa som lysar upp och då försvinnar.

Jag är fingar av gry.
Jag är guldet.
Jag strolar inte
Jag gnistra inte
Jag lysa.
Natten följer efter mig varhelst jag åk.
Höljd av svart mörkret min mantel.
Jag är hopp det spelar ingen roll hur länge natten
kan vara.
Återvända jag.

The Wanderer

You're the reason I'm still here
And haven't wandered far away
I often think of running
But because of you, I stay
One day you'll be gone
And though I may look back
It'll only be for a moment
They can't stop me once I've packed
I am the traveler
The wanderer
On my weary way
But because you're in this moment
Here I choose to stay

Just One Day

If I had one more day to spend
However I chose
To climb the highest mountain
To smell the sweetest rose
To conquer my demons
To travel to space
Of all the sights to see
I'd choose that place
Where you stand by my side
You take my hand
It doesn't matter if it's here
Or some distant land
With your hand in mine
Forever I'll stay
I'd give everything up
For just that one day

Standing By Someone

I've often been looked down on
And ridiculed for being young
Well now I'm all grown-up
And those mocking have changed their song

Suddenly my intelligence
Is looking less like a game
Now that I'm on "their level"
They have respect when they speak my name

It's funny, how they see me now
Their whole outlook has changed
But I'm choosing to stick with the people
Who've treated me the same

While others stood and laughed
Few were by my side
And now those who were laughing are realizing
That's not the tactic they should have tried

Yes, I'm all grown-up now
Strong, independent, and free

And now that I'm choosing to stand by someone
I'm choosing someone who stood by me

Effort

If not with ease, like nature, poetry comes
It is seen as fake
If it requires effort to keep love alive
It is said that it will easily shake

But I have seen the poet ponder
In the deepest realms of thought
And the strongest steel there's ever been
Is the Damascus, folded while still hot

While effortlessness may seem pretty
Compared to an uphill climb
I'd rather fight to hold one's hand
And know they'll fight to hold mine

Home

We talked so much about our futures
What we'd each do when we got home
You came back
Now I'm gone

I'm so glad I got to see you
So glad I got to hear your name
But it made it oh, so much harder
For me to have to turn and walk away
It was one thing
When we said someday we'd come home
But that's not either of our homes anymore

Our families are still there
While we up and roam
Wandering the world
Trying to find home
They're still our families
The blood we've always known
But now it's our turn
To try and make our own

We talked so much about the future
If only we'd have known

Here we are in the future
Wandering without a home

Otherworldly

The rosy glow
Streaming pink and orange
The fingers of gold bursting brilliantly forth
But there is a time in which glory and splendor
Have no place or meaning
In the night
Where the only light comes from the pale
shining moon and twinkling stars
Where the regal creatures roam
The darkness encasing the noise of the world
Leaving only the otherworldly

Grandfather's Hands

Covered in calluses and wrinkles, each tells a
story.
His nails are cracked, but always clean
Perpetually helping are the hands of the man
who does so much.
He teaches me to do the jobs he no longer can,
His hands switching from quickly shelling
pecans with rough hands,
To softly, warmly holding mine in an instant.
His hands are as strong and sure as a river, yet
still gentle.
Can you teach me to have hands like yours,
Grandpa?
"I can show you, but you must be willing to
learn."

Silver Tears

Shine on in the stars, brother
Shine in the lights above
You're free and clear of weakness
Now look over the things you love
You shone in life brighter than the sun
Now that you're gone
The stars are joined by one of their own
Silver teardrops
Water the world
And your strength keeps living on

Self Righteous

Losing faith as I walk down the street
Losing patience with every person that I meet
I needed a break
So I walked out the door
I can't do this anymore
Why is everyone so
Self righteous
Caught up in their stupid pride
Everyone is oh so
Self righteous
Either that or all the humble ones hide
The world is drowning in
Puffed up people
Suffocating in their claims to fame
Millions of bodies
Laughing and mocking
Few win, though we all play the game

Publicity

I'm catching up on the news when
An article flashes across my screen
A famous singer and an actor have broken up

"For the publicity"
"May have ruined his chances for that film"
"What is she going to write about him"

Can't they just be?
Let them figure themselves out and then include
the world, if they so choose?
Like normal people
But wait
The world does the same thing to normal people,
too

"Just wanted the attention"
"Took a different job for her"
"What does she have to say for herself?"

As if they answer to you
As if perfect relationships just fall from trees
Like we, the struggling young adults of our day
Aren't trying hard enough

But we can barely begin to figure ourselves out
And then our relationship
When everyone wants to know
What happened
They judge, no matter what we do

And then,
And then,
And then,
They obliviously ask
Why we're still single

Orange Glitter

Orange glitter
Didn't mean to make you cry
But the memories are flooding me
And I can't just keep standing by
You were there for me when all else ignored
But I can't help you if won't stop barring the
door

Gone From Me

Wrapped up in the whispers
Shrouded in the smoke
I closed my eyes and listened
As those fateful words he spoke
"I love you" fell first from his lips
"But I don't want you to see me so.
I love you
That's why you need to go."
Many times I've looked back
And replayed that ghostly scene
For now he is no longer
My love, now gone from me

I Suppose

I suppose you could say all the words we have
Have already been used
We are just rearranging them
In the hopes of creating something new
Our songs have already been sung
The melodies falling into endless cycles
I suppose you could say
We have already loved
And lived
And died

One could say that.
However
I choose to see
That I am doing everything
For the very
First
Time

Violin

A violin case in hand
The world lies at your feet
The strains of unearthly music
Echo across the seas

The steady pull of the bow
The gentle hum of the strings
The forest itself stops to listen
And the birds cease to sing

The power you hold in your hands
Is fickle and tries to run
But you, my dear, have tamed it
And before the rising sun

You play for the world your sorrows
You show them all how you feel
Coaxing a haunting melody
Otherworldly and surreal

Dead of Night

Silver whisper
Stage fright
Evening dew
Dead of night

Distant moon
Shining high
Foreign stars
Breathless sigh

Wishful thoughts
Days alone
Wandering dreams
Coming home

Endless shadows
Mind alight
Evening dew
Dead of night

Letter

faded parchment
crinkled page
ink worn with time
rubbed bare with age
whispered promises
last goodbyes
tear spots on paper
long since dried
write a letter
to my love
hope she can read it
up above

Bittersweet

The warmth of the sunshine on my face
As the breeze washes over my skin
Crisp is the air that I breathe
As I let it all rush back in

It's been a while since I last saw you
And so much has changed
It's been a while since we moved on
And we both moved away

It's not that I didn't love you
Quite the opposite, actually
And as I stand here
All the memories coming back to me
Are bittersweet

I'm back for a visit so I came to see
That magical place we'd go
It was a shelter for you and me
Where we always came back, no matter where
we roamed

It's been quite some time
And as I think on all we went through
I realize time hasn't changed a thing

I'm still in love with you

It's not that I didn't love you
Quite the opposite, actually
And as I stand here
All the memories coming back to me
Are bittersweet

We had a beautiful time together
No one else has ever made me feel the same
You made me love you with all the little things,
darling
You made me smile every time I heard you say
my name

Time was the cruelest thing
That pulled us apart
I want you to know that I still love you
No matter where you are

It's not that I didn't love you
Quite the opposite, actually
And as I stand here
All the memories coming back to me
Are bittersweet

So, darling, maybe while I'm here
We could meet and talk for an hour or two
And if I told you how I feel

...what would you do?

The past is done
It's all faded to memory
But perhaps we could move on
And this time it won't be
Bittersweet

Paint the Sky

Paint the sky
Burn the moon
Turn the sun to gold
Let your grasp loosen
Feel your fingertips slide
Release the hand that you hold

Silence the morning
Bid adieu to the night
Withhold your mournful cry
Don't let the teardrops fall
As you kiss it all goodbye

www.ingramcontent.com/pod-product-compliance
Lightning Source LLC
LaVergne TN
LVHW021345200726

843509LV00014B/2684